■ *Please return by the*
latest date stamped
below to avoid a charge
■ *You may renew by*
telephoning any library
in the borough. Please
quote the number on
the barcode label below

Barnet Libraries

1 045068 05

Teach Yourself Lead Guitar.

By Steve Tarshis.

045068

AMSCO

5.95

Photo Credits

Barry Wetcher   technical photos
Herb Wise   9
Mark MacLaren   12, 30, 51, 59
The Photo Reserve/Vito Palmisano   62

Series Editor: Mark Michaels
Cover Design: Pearce Marchbank

ⓒ Amsco Music Publishing Company, 1978
A Division of Music Sales Corporation, New York
All Rights Reserved

Distributed throughout the world by Music Sales Corporation:
24 East 22nd Street, NY 10010, New York USA
8/9 Frith Street, London, W1V 5TZ, England
27 Clarendon Street, Artarmon, Sydney NSW 2064

Printed and bound in Great Britain at
The Camelot Press Ltd, Southampton

787.6107

BOROUGH   T

G   6/91   CB   £5.95

860018954

OF11701951

Contents

Foreword

This is a book about lead guitar. At certain points in their development all guitarists reach a stage at which they feel frustrated. They've gotten a few things down, but something's missing. Perhaps they don't know how to begin to play lead guitar. Or, they've gotten a good start but "it just doesn't sound like the record."

You may know in your mind what you want to hear, but getting those fingers to respond is another matter.

I hope the ideas to follow will touch off a thinking process and give you material to work with to create your own style.

You don't have to read music because charts and tablature, as well as written music, have been used. But I hope that you'll try to get into it. Reading is a tool. It can put you in touch with thousands of other musicians and they all have their own story.

To get the most out of the book, go slowly and think about how the information relates to what you already know. Some things may take a while to sink in. But if you're playing and studying all the time, you'll be surprised at the progress you can make.

Students always ask, "How long before I become a really great player?" I always reply that the more hours the guitar is in your hands, the better you'll get. So be persistent, and above all, enjoy it.

How to hold the guitar

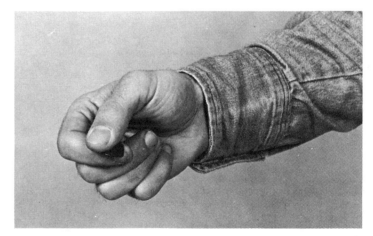

How to hold the pick

Fundamentals

Before starting our study of lead guitar, it's important to talk a little about the rudiments of music. Learning to read music is not difficult. Notation is the way in which musicians communicate to one another, so let's learn the language. We'll use two methods of communication, traditional musical notation, and guitar tablature. It's not necessary for you to know both to use this book. Either one will do. We'll also look at some written-out rhythms that we'll be using.

Let's look at traditional notation first.

On paper, music sounds are represented by written symbols called *notes*. The notes are written on a *staff* which consists of five lines and the four spaces between them.

There are seven notes in the musical alphabet, A, B, C, D, E, F, and G. These seven notes are repeated over and over again. The location of the notes on the staff shows their pitch.

The spaces between the barlines are *measures*.

The names of the notes contained on the lines are, starting with the first line: E, G, B, D, F (memory trick: Every Good Boy Does Fine). The notes in the spaces are, starting with the first space: F, A, C, E (spells the word "face").

In music notation the *treble clef* is always placed at the beginning of the staff when writing music for guitar.

Notes which are higher or lower in pitch than those on the staff are written below and above the staff with *leger lines*.

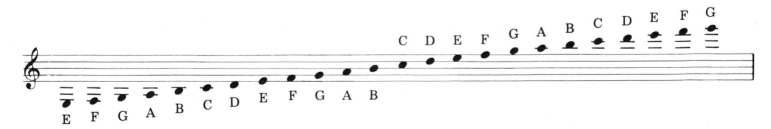

Sharps and Flats

Although there are only seven notes in the musical alphabet, there are twelve pitches in the musical octave, from which we draw all the notes. The other pitches are derived by the use of sharps and flats. Sharps raise the pitch one half step (one fret on the guitar) and flats lower the pitch by one half step. A sharp or a flat remains in effect for one measure. A natural sign cancels the sharp or flat. Sharps, flats, and natural signs are called *accidentals*.

Sharp—♯
Flat—♭
Natural—♮

Time

Rhythm and *meter* are two of the most essential aspects of the art of music. Just think, as a musician you are trying to control the flow of time, quite a heavy thought. Coming down to earth, however, the notation of time control is accomplished in this way. The formation of a written note indicates its duration—how long the note lasts. This is relative to the *tempo*. The tempo is the rate of speed at which the music moves.

In $\frac{4}{4}$ meter, a *whole note* receives four beats. A *half note* gets two beats. A *quarter note* is the basic unit, getting one beat. *Eighth notes* receive half a beat each, and *sixteenth notes* receive a quarter of a beat. A $\frac{4}{4}$ indication (*time signature*) at the beginning of a piece of music shows that there are four quarter note beats per measure of music. Most rock music is written in $\frac{4}{4}$.

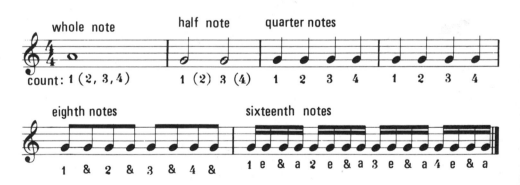

Rests

Rests indicate a breathing space in the music. Each note value has its equivalent rest as shown below.

Ties

Ties are used to connect note values, as shown below.

Tablature

Tablature is a system of music notation that has been developed specifically for guitarists. It takes place on a six line staff, each line representing one of the six strings of the guitar. A number indicates which fret on the guitar is to be fingered. Rests and other musical symbols are basically the same. All the music in this book will be written in both notations. I strongly recommend that both systems be learned, although a knowledge of either one will suffice. Either one can be learned as you go along in the book.

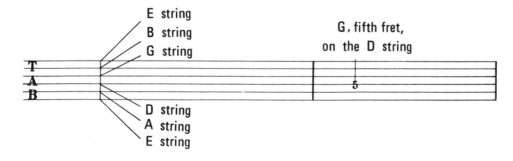

Traditional Notation and Guitar Tablature

The Blues Scale

Strange as it may seem, the single most important tool of the lead guitarist is a simple scale containing only five notes. All guitarists spend years with these notes, bending and twisting them, always finding new ways to interpret them. In fact, this simple scale is the basis for the music of a surprising number of diverse cultures around the world.

Here is the blues scale in the key of G. We'll start with the first four strings of the guitar in third position.*

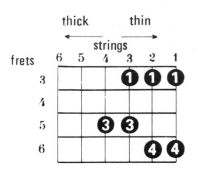

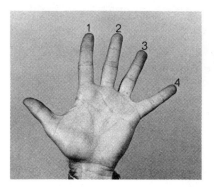

The numbers on the chart correspond with your left hand fingers as shown.

The five notes in a G blues scale are G, B♭, C, D and F. Notated, they look like this.

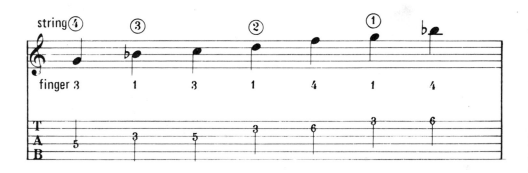

Third position means beginning on the third fret.

8

Chord Progression

Let's see how these notes may be used in a common rock chord progression. First, play through the chords and try to get the sound of them in your head.

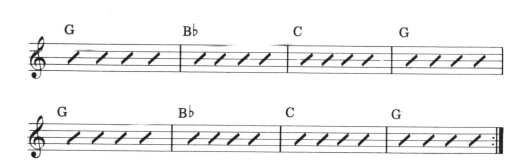

John McLaughlin

Here's a lead that may be played against these chords. After you've practiced it, try playing this lead with a friend playing the chords. Friendship aside, a cassette tape machine is an excellent tool for any musician. If you have one, record the progression a few times and then play lead while the recording accompanies you.

Practice the above to get familiar with the fingerings and notation.

Here's another lead with the same notes, same chords.

*This accent over the note (>) means hit the note hard!

Now, try some leads on your own using these notes and the same chord progression. You will notice that the more authoritatively you play, the better you will sound. You should give some thought to style and experiment with different sounds. For example, a hard rock sound may be obtained by turning up the amp or using a distortion device. Small amps turned up sound great. If your amp has a master volume control, turn that down and turn the other volume control up. For a funk, or R&B sound, a jazzier approach may be used. Strive here for a clean sound, use the bright switch if the amp has one. Turn up the treble. Try all kinds of sounds and variations. Your sound is as important and personal as the notes you play.

Note: Pay special attention to the fourth finger. The pinky is often neglected and your muscles there probably need development. Playing well is often a matter of having strong fingers.

Chuck Berry

Extending the Blues Scale Downward

Let's try extending the G blues scale to the lower strings, but staying in third position.

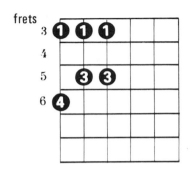

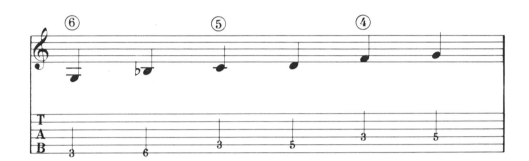

Low Note Riffs

These low notes are great for riffs. *Riffs* are repeated patterns that often form the basis for a song. Sometimes the lead player plays these riffs with the bass player to get an especially powerful sound.

Here are some low note riffs using the G blues scale. Play each one several times.

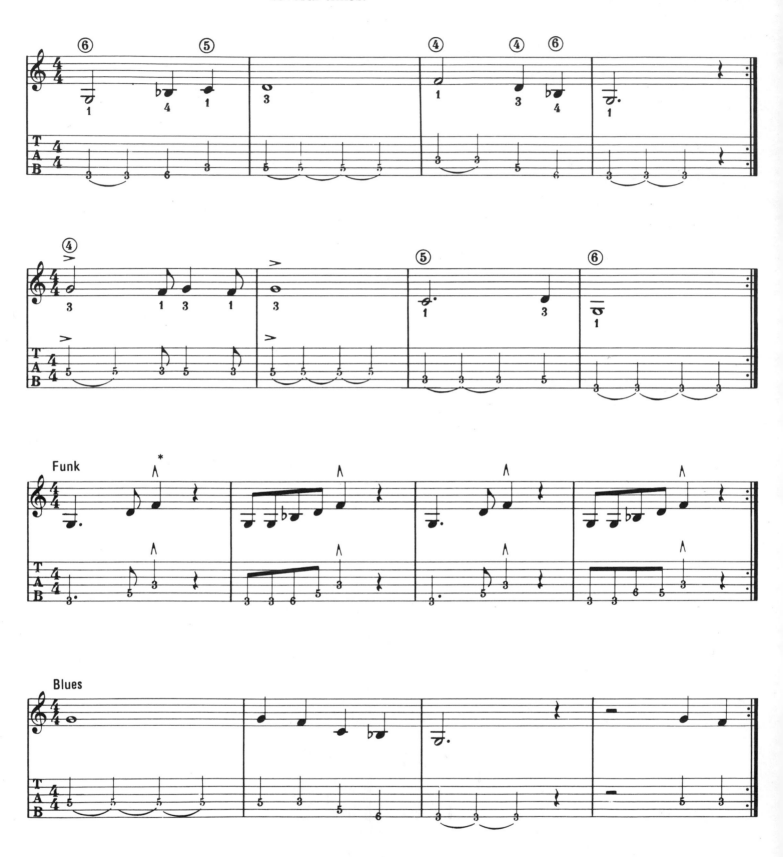

*A hat (∧) over a note means "choke" the note, or play it short by immediately removing the left hand after striking it.

The Whole Blues Scale

Here's the complete G blues scale in third position:

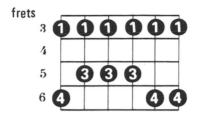

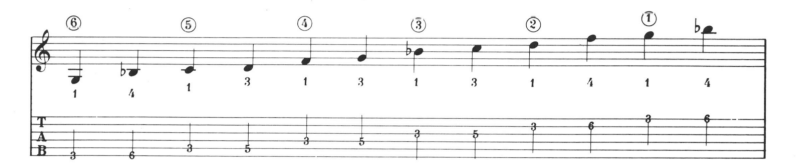

Leads

Let's try a bluesy, laid-back lead. Play through it—just chords first, then notes. Try improvising on your own once you get the feel. Use these notes in as many ways as you can.

B.B. King

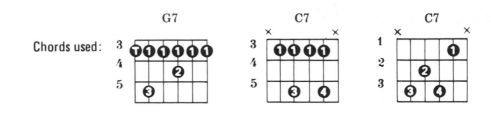

Chords used:

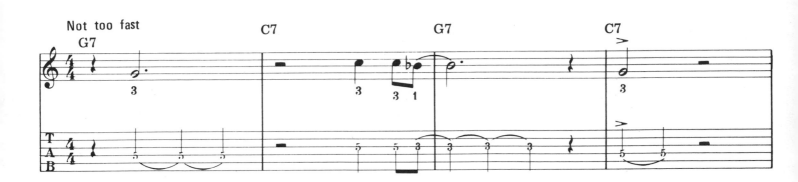

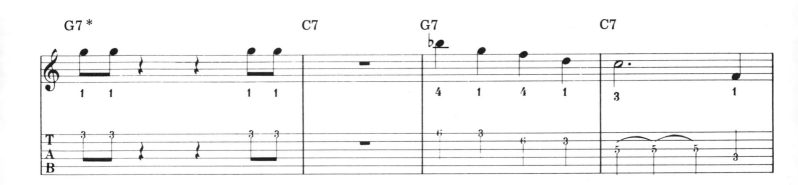

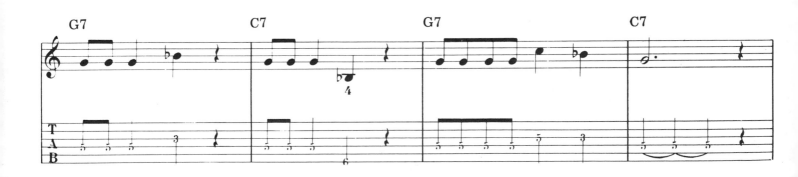

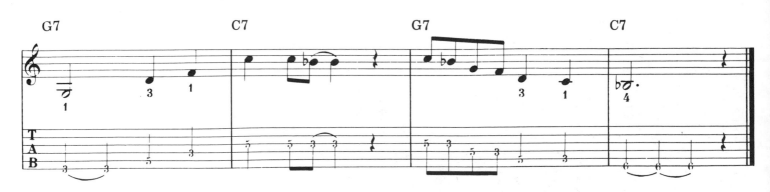

*Repeated notes are often effective, as is the use of silence in the next measure.

Here's another chord progression to try. A more melodic effect is achieved, still using the same notes. Again, try to practice each example in these steps: (1) Play the chords. (2) Play the lead as written until you're familiar with it. (3) Improvise your own lead, if possible with a friend or tape recorder playing the chords.

Extending the Blues Scale Upward

Positions

We are now going to find the notes in the G blues scale in a higher register, or higher pitch. These new notes occur in the sixth position. The sixth fret, which was covered by the fourth finger in third position, will now be covered by the first finger. Logically, the second finger is now playing the notes on the seventh fret, and the third finger is covering the eighth fret. The fourth finger will cover the ninth fret and stretch for the tenth.

Third Position:

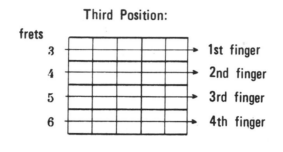

Sixth position:

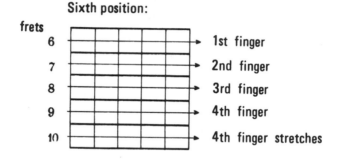

The G blues scale in sixth position is found in the following way. Play the note G (in the third position) on the first string.

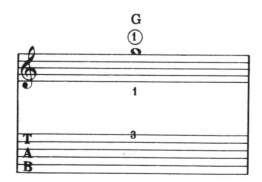

Now, find this note five frets higher, on the second string. Same note, different string (second), different fret (eighth), different position (sixth).

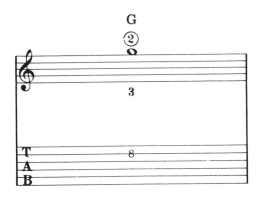

This is how we anchor into the new position. On the fretboard:

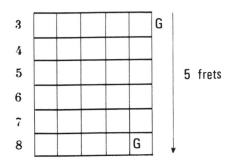

The notes in sixth position:

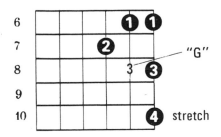

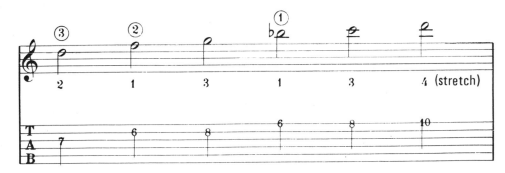

Leads

Here is a lead using the new notes. These higher notes are excellent for "stinging" solos.

Here's another progression. Study the chords and the notes to see how they work together. Don't forget to try your own leads after you work out the examples. Be sure to use the correct fingering. Don't neglect that fourth finger—build it up.

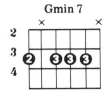

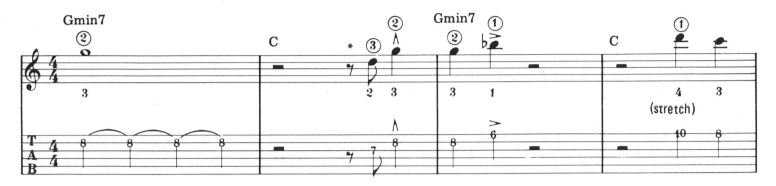

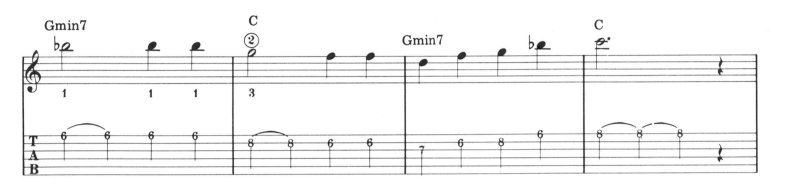

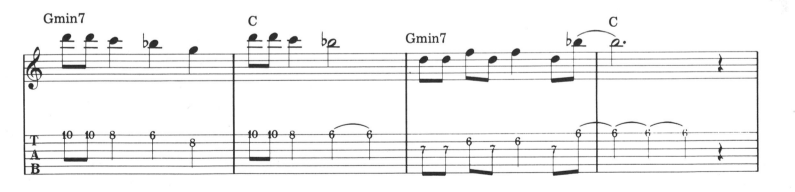

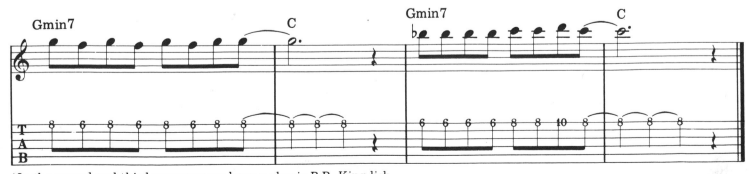

*In the second and third measures we have a classic B.B. King lick.

Scale Exercises

Before going on, let's review some of the information we've covered. I want you to really learn the two scale positions we've used so that your fingers can start thinking on their own.

Let's talk a bit about practicing. We can take a tip from classical and jazz musicians who know that the constant and regular practice of scale exercises is some of the most efficient practicing you can do. You can learn the notes, build your endurance, strengthen your fingers, develop your rhythmic sense, train your ear and build your speed all at the same time. So let's practice those scales.

We'll start in third position.

G Blues Scale Exercise

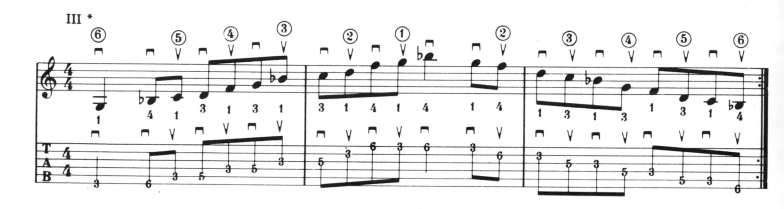

The small marks over each note indicate how each note should be picked with your right hand.

⊓ = down-stroke V = up-stroke

This technique of alternate picking is essential for developing speed and fluidity.

Start playing the scale slowly. Your objective now is to play each note cleanly and evenly, and to learn to utilize alternate picking. You can also try the scale with all down-strokes, or all up-strokes to achieve different sounds and inflections. Perhaps you have realized that by learning one scale position you are learning many more. For example, by moving from third to fifth position, but keeping the same note pattern, we get the A blues scale. The fingering is exactly the same as the G blues scale, but we are now working on the fifth, seventh and eighth frets, using the notes A, C, D, E and G.

*A Roman numeral placed at the top of the staff will indicate the position on the neck. III = third position.

A Blues Scale Exercise

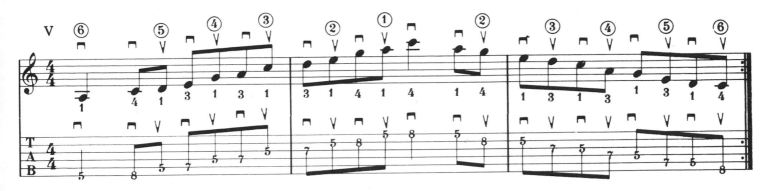

Now, let's move up the neck to the eighth fret to play the C blues scale. The notes here are C, E♭, F, G and B♭.

C Blues Scale Exercise

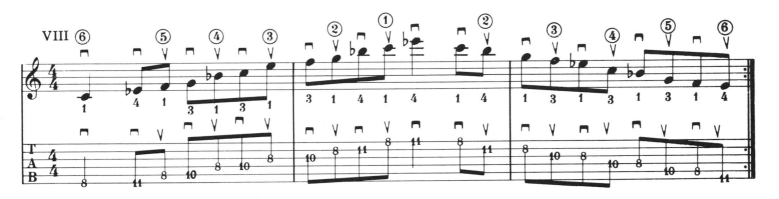

Practice these over and over every day. Don't just play mechanically. *Hear* each note, really listen. Be critical; try to get just the sound you want. Play these scales in as many different ways as you can think of—loud, soft, long notes, short notes—but *always* play in time, no matter how fast or slow you start. (Playing slow is often more difficult than playing fast.)   Here is a scale exercise using the sixth position G blues scale that we learned.

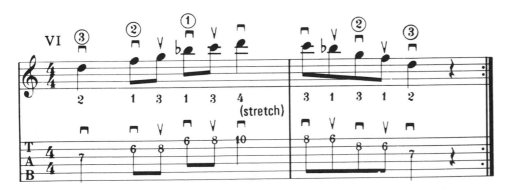

Moving to eighth position, with the same fingering, we get an A blues scale.

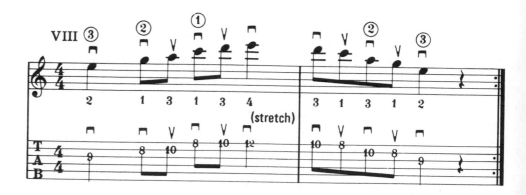

Now we take the same fingering all the way up to eleventh position and get the C blues scale. Don't be afraid of leger lines. If you're not sure of the notes, take the time now to learn them. Otherwise, you'll always pass over them and miss some good music.

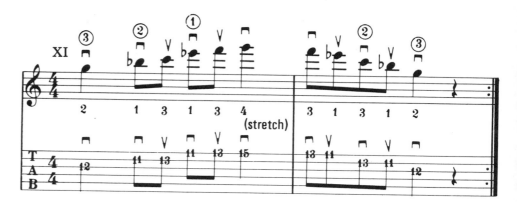

I've written out each fingering in three keys, but an excellent exercise is to take each fingering and move up the neck as far as you can go and then move back down again. For example, play the G blues scale up and down in third position. Then move to the fourth position for the A♭ blues scale. Then go to the fifth, sixth, and so on as far up the neck as you can go. Then come back down.

Repeat this procedure using the second fingering we learned, G blues scale in sixth position.

Practice these exercises every day as much as possible.

Positions, Scale Names, Fingerings

Position	Fingering One	Fingering Two
I	F blues scale	D blues scale
II	F♯ /G♭	E♭
III	G	E
IV	G♯ , A♭	F
V	A	G♭/F♯
VI	B♭	G
VII	B	A♭/G♯
VIII	C	A
IX	D♭/C♯	B♭
X	D	B
XI	E♭	C
XII	E	D♭/C♯
XIII	F	D
XIV	F♯ /G♭	E♭
XV	G	E
XVI	G♯ /A♭	F
XVII	A	F♯ /G♭

Bends

By now you should have a pretty good idea of the notes you can use to build a good lead. From listening to other guitarists and recordings you probably realize that some kind of coloration is necessary to bring the notes alive. One commonly used device is the technique of *bending* notes.

Let's look at some bends in the third position blues scale. Here's the first.

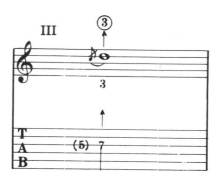

An arrow (↑) over a note, will indicate a bend. The small note (*grace note*) shows where the note originates, in this case the C on the fifth fret, third string. This is the note on which you place your finger. The written D is the pitch you bend the note up to. To execute a bend, finger the grace note (in tablature the grace note is in parentheses), strike that note with your right hand, and *immediately* bend the note upward to the next pitch. This is a very physical and expressive movement that takes a bit of practice. No two guitarists play a bend exactly the same way, and you should listen to recordings as much as possible for ideas and inspiration. And of course, practice, practice, practice.

Light gauge or extra light gauge strings are best for bending notes.

Here is a lick using this bend.

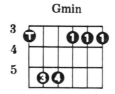

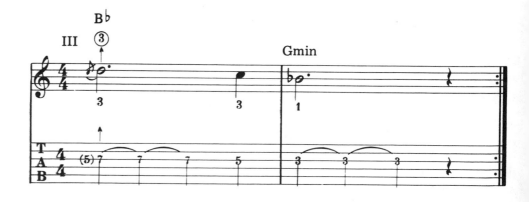

In the next bend, the fourth finger raises the F on the second string up to G.

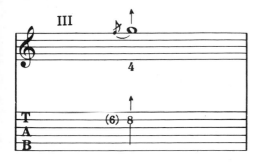

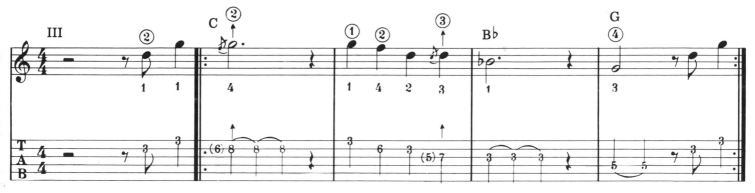

One other bend in this same fingering and position pushes the Bb on the first string, sixth fret, up to the pitch C.

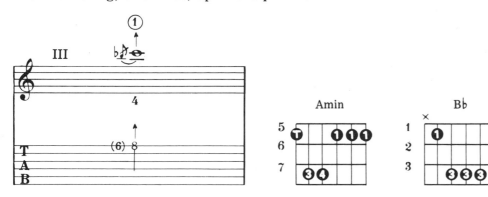

Try this run.

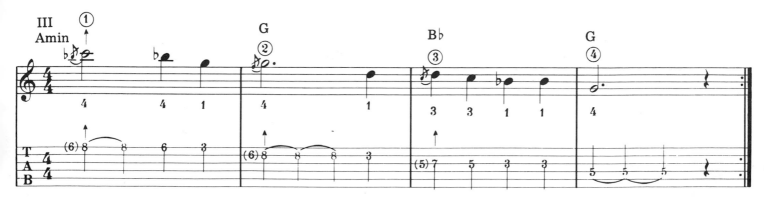

You should practice these runs over and over (use the repeat signs!) preferably with someone playing the chords. Make sure to try your own licks using these ideas. Build up those fingers; they have to be strong to control bending properly.

*Repeat signs (‖: :‖) call for the repetition of the music enclosed by them.

So far, all of these bends have been in the third position G blues scale. But we can change keys, maintaining the same fingering, by moving up and down the fretboard in the same way we practiced scales. Try this lead in A, fifth position.

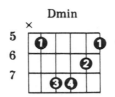

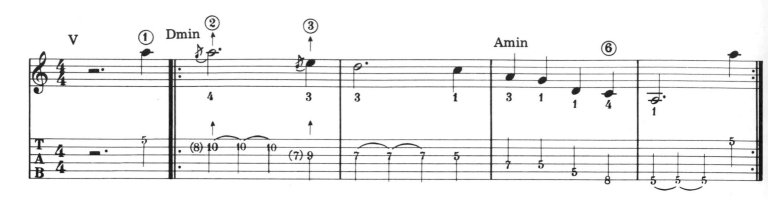

In C, eighth position, here's a Chuck Berry lick.

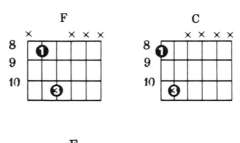

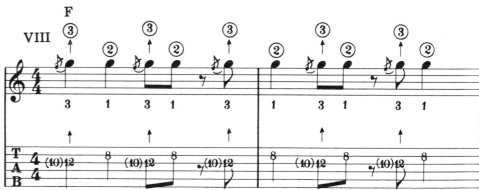

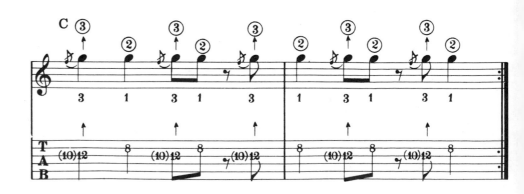

A very useful bend occurs within the second fingering we learned. In the G blues fingering in sixth position the C on the first string, eighth fret may be bent up to a D.

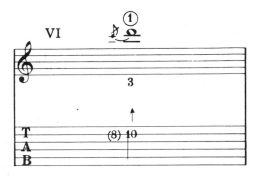

Here's a run.

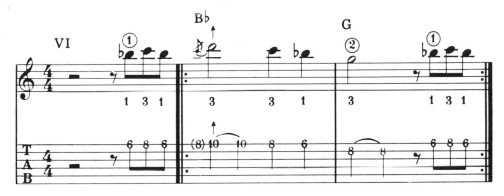

The same fingering in A, eighth position.

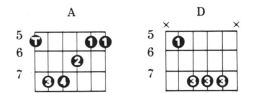

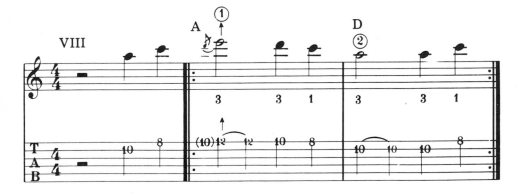

In E, third position.

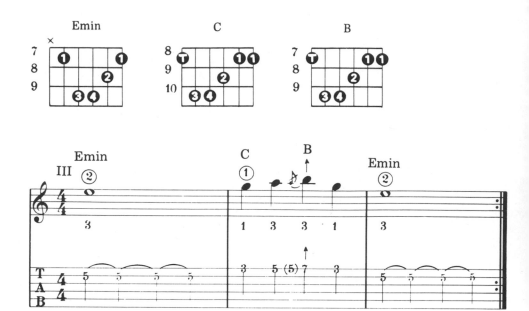

Peter Frampton

Combining Positions

At this point we can greatly expand the possibilities for lead work by combining the two basic fingerings we've learned. In G, these are:

Fingering One:

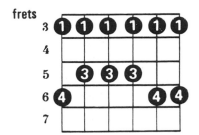

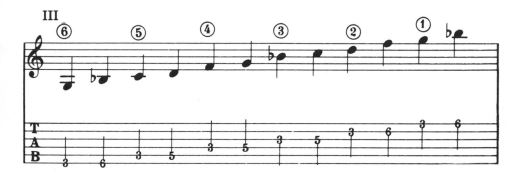

Fingering Two:

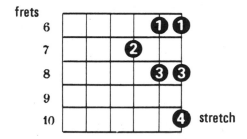

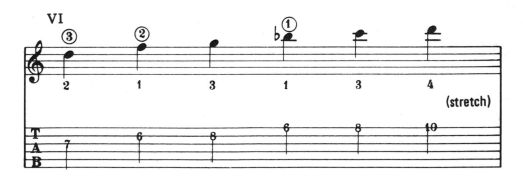

Leads

In the following leads, the Roman numerals will indicate when to switch positions, and which position you should be playing in. Take the time to work out the examples carefully, and soon you'll be able to play your own leads up and down the neck. Pay attention to the chords that go with the notes. Play through the progressions several times and try to get the sound in your head before you tackle the notes. Once you learn the solo, get someone to play the chords while you play lead. This is very important. Don't forget to try your own leads over these progressions using the techniques of combining positions and bending notes.

We'll start, as usual, in the key of G.

Let's re-center to the key of A, using the same basic fingerings but moving them up two frets. Fingering One will be in fifth position. We will combine this with Fingering Two in eighth position.

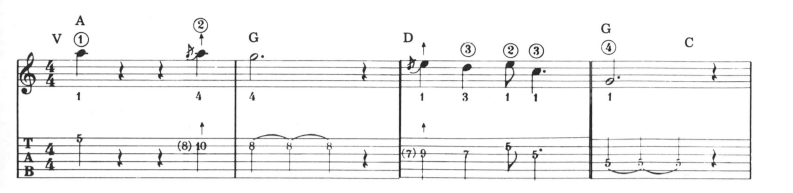

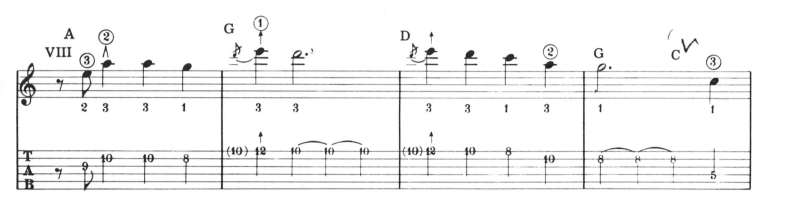

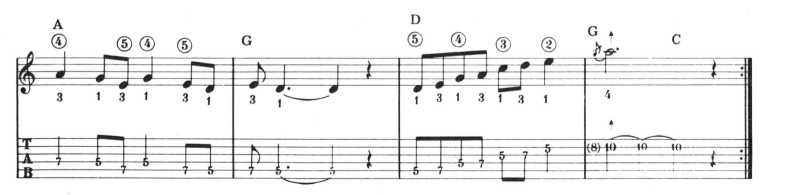

Some funk in C. Fingering One in eighth position, Fingering Two in eleventh position.

34

Scale Runs

Practice these leads and then try your own in various keys. The following is a scale run exercise that will help you to make the transition between the two fingerings we've learned.

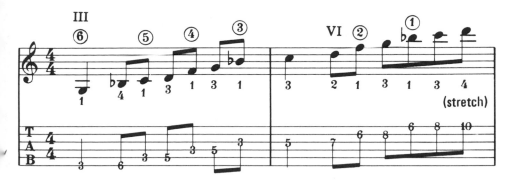

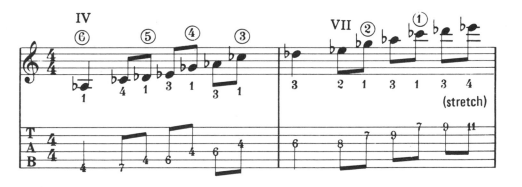

The same run, same fingering, up a half step (one fret) to A♭.

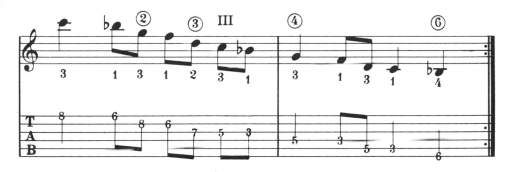

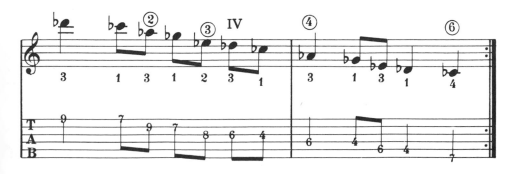

Now move up another fret to A.

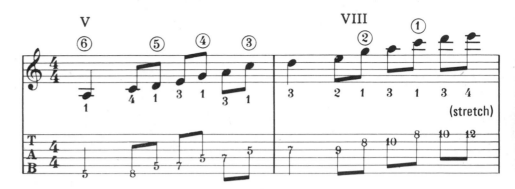

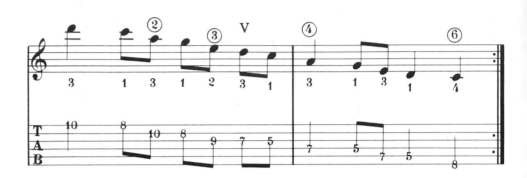

Practice this run by moving it up a half step at a time. Go up the neck as far as you can, then come back down. This exercise will really help you learn how to combine positions and increase your ability to get around the neck.

Blues Solos

Although we've been dealing with the blues scale, we haven't yet dealt with an out and out blues chord progression. This series of chord relationships and the notes that are played over it (the blues scale you've studied) have been the basis of expression for musicians throughout this century, bridging all styles from jazz to hard rock.

Here are some blues solos in G and Bb. Pay special attention to the chord accompaniment and to the phrasing (the space between the notes).

These chords, used in the next few examples, may be new to you.

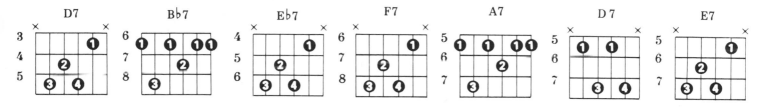

G Blues, Fingering One: third position
      Fingering Two: sixth position.

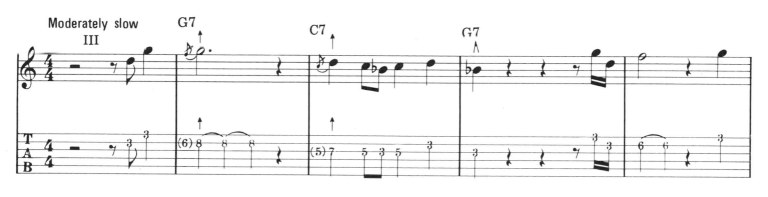

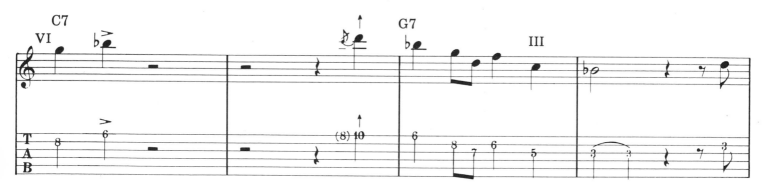

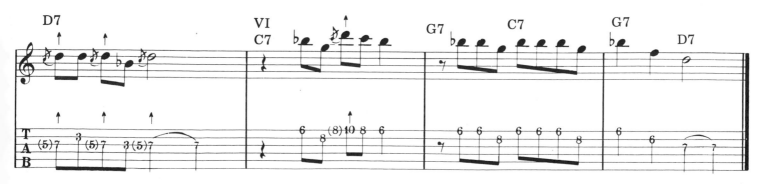

B♭ Blues, Fingering One: sixth position
Fingering Two: ninth position.

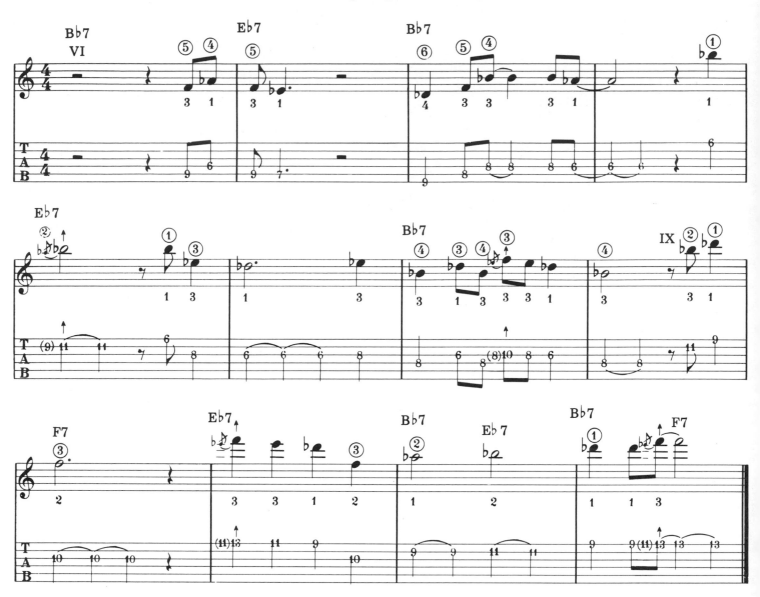

Try your own leads against these progressions. Then try some solos against the progressions below. The correct fingerings and positions are given.

F Blues, Fingering One: first position
Fingering Two: fourth position.

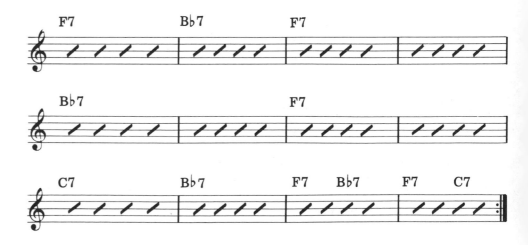

A Blues, Fingering One: fifth position
    Fingering Two: eighth position.

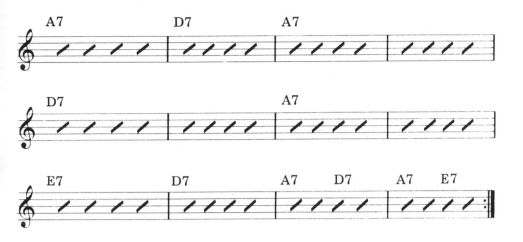

_____

Quiz

Can you figure out the right chords for these keys?

C, Fingering One: eighth position
    Fingering Two: eleventh position.

E (tricky), Fingering One: twelfth position
    Fingering Two: third position.

_____

Other Uses of the Blues Scale

If you've studied the relationship between the chords in the examples and the blues scales that went with them, you probably have some idea of what notes you can play against different kinds of chord progressions. However, there may be some blanks in your thinking, so let's try to standardize some of the uses of the blues scale.

As we've just seen, the most obvious use of the blues scale is against a blues progression, as in the previous section. There are many chord progressions similar to, but not exactly the same as, the basic blues progression. A blues scale may always be used in these progressions.

Funk

Funk music often uses blues-based chords (G7, C7, D7, etc.) as in the following examples. The G blues scale is used in this progression, Fingering Two, sixth position.

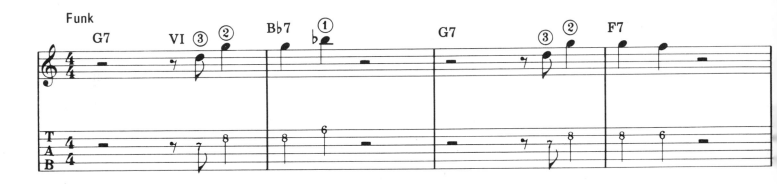

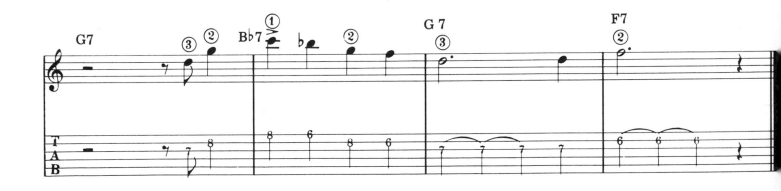

The C blues scale, Fingering One, eighth position.

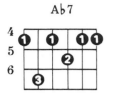

Minor

Another use of the blues scale is against minor chords. Use the scale with the same key name as the chord around which the progression is built. Often the first chord, the last chord, or the chord that appears most often is the key chord. A G blues scale may be used against the following progression built around a G minor chord.

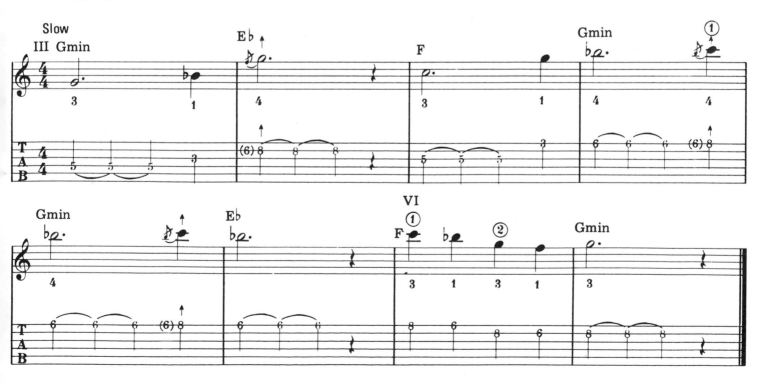

Use the A blues scale against this next progression. Try playing with a rock feel, then maybe with a soul or disco flavor.

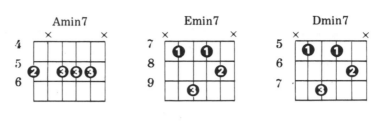

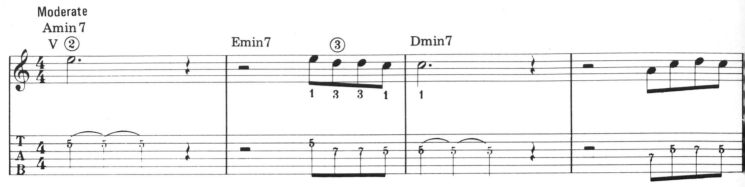

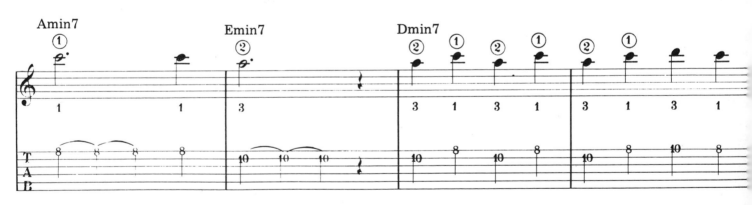

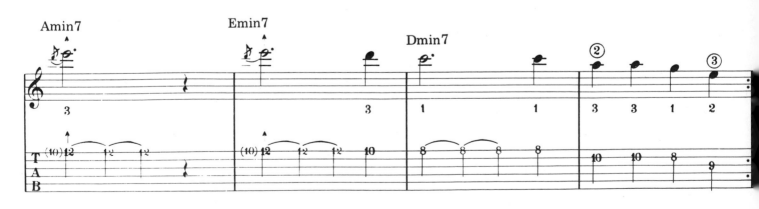

The Related Major

As you may realize by now, the blues scale has many different uses. Despite the name we've given it, its uses are not just limited to blues progressions. Rock guitarists have always used this scale as their most useful tool. The same can be said for jazz, funk and country players.

This brings us to one of the most important uses of our scale. We've seen the blues scale used against progressions centered around the chords of the same key name. For example, a G blues scale for a G minor progression and an A blues scale for an A7 progression, etc. But sometimes a scale may be used in a progression that has no chords of its own name in it. In other words, a lead player may be using a G blues scale against a progression with no G chords of any kind in it. When this happens they are most likely playing in the key that is the related major of the scale they are using.

To explain this, a little theory is necessary.

Chromatic Scale

In music, the distance between notes is measured in *half steps* and *whole steps*. On your guitar, a half step is equal to one fret and a whole step is equal to two frets. The distance between G and Ab is a half step; between G and A, a whole step. Look at the chart below. It lists all the notes by half step. Since there are only twelve notes, the cycle repeats itself at every octave. When we speak of all the notes laid out by half step like this, we call it the *chromatic scale*.

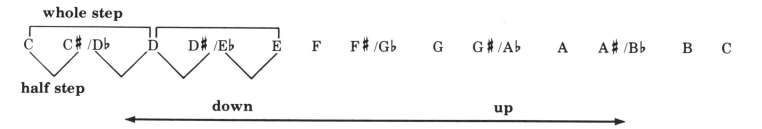

Except for B-C and E-F, the sharp of a lower note equals the flat of its alphabetical upper neighbor. Notes with this relationship (C# and Db for example) are called *enharmonic*.

The related major key of a given blues scale is three half steps up. This means that the related major key of a G blues scale is Bb. The related major scale of an A blues scale is C. Check this for yourself on the chart.

Now, suppose you have a chord progression and you want to know what blues scale you can use to play over it. If you can find out what major key the chords are in, then you may move *down* three half steps to find the right blues scale.

In the next example, we have a progression that is in the major key of Bb. Moving down three half steps (look at the chromatic scale chart or, better yet, do it on your guitar) we get G. A G blues scale may be used against a Bb major progression. This device is frequently used in country and country-rock music. Here the G blues scale is used, Fingering One, third position. Notice that the home note (the one used to complete a phrase or resolve an idea) is Bb.

The scale and fingering is exactly the same as in previous examples where G was the home note. The difference is in the chords. The main idea here is that the same scale may be used in completely different settings. The home note changes according to the progression.

Major Progression

A G blues scale is used against the following progression in the major key of B♭. Try using a country or country rock feeling.

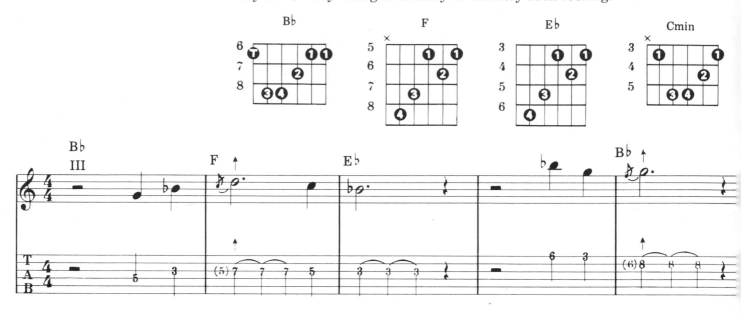

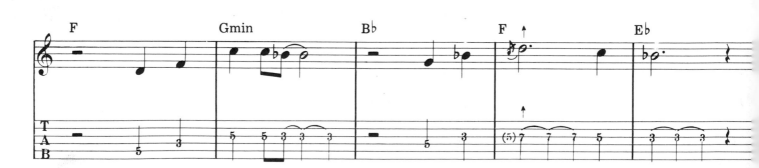

The chords in this progression all belong to the key of B♭. The G blues scale is used to play over these chords. Make sure to try your own leads using the G blues scale while a friend plays the chords.

Blues Scales and Related Major Keys

The chart below will help you understand the chord/scale relationship we've been talking about. It lists all the major keys and the blues scales to which they are related. The chords that are most likely to appear in each major key are also listed.

Blues Scale	Major Key	Chords Used in this Key
G	B♭	B♭, Cmin, Dmin, E♭, F, Gmin, Adim,
A♭	B	B, C#min, D#min, E, F#, G#min, A#dim
A	C	C, Dmin, Emin, F, G, Amin, Bdim
B♭	C#	C#, D#min, E#min, F#, G#, A#min, B#dim
B	D	D, Emin, F#min, G, A, Bmin, C#min
C	E♭	E♭, Fmin, Gmin, A♭, B♭, Cmin, Ddim
C#	E	E, F#min, G#min, A, B, C#min, D#dim
D	F	F, Gmin, Amin, B♭, C, Dmin, Edim
E♭	F#	F#, G#min, A#min, B, C#, D#min, E#dim
E	G	G, Amin, Bmin, C, D, Emin, F#dim
F	A♭	A♭, B♭min, Cmin, D♭, E♭, Fmin, Gdim
F#	A	A, Bmin, C#min, D, E, F#min, G#dim

Sevenths

The chords listed for each key in the chart are all major, minor or diminished. But each chord has a seventh chord that is an extension of itself. One more note (the seventh) may be added, and you may find these chords in progressions over which you want to play lead. This presents no real problem. For example, in the key of G we have listed under chords used: G, Amin, Bmin, C, D, Emin and F# dim. The seventh chords that may appear in this key are Gmaj7, Amin7, Bmin7, Cmaj7, D7, Emin7 and F# dim7. The seventh chords in the major key of A are Amaj7, Bmin7, C#min7, Dmaj7, E7, F# min7, and G# dim7.

Let's analyze this next chord progression.

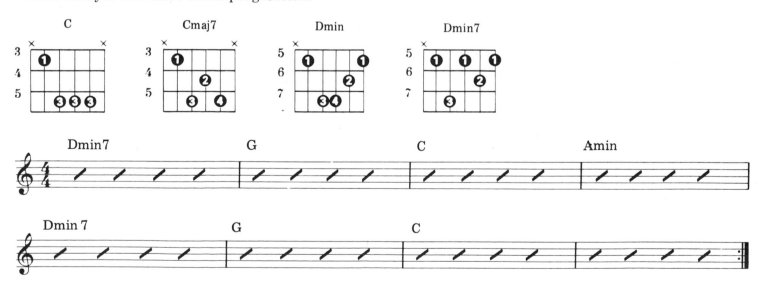

Play the chords through and try to get an idea of the sound of them. With a tape recorder or friend, try out some ideas for lead while the chords are played. You may find the notes you want in this way. It's the best way to practice improvising. Try to see if you can find the blues scale that fits.

Looking at the chart (Blues Scales and Related Major Keys) find the key that contains all of the chords in the progression. If the key is C major, the related blues scale (the one that is three half steps down the chromatic scale) is A. Practice and experience will develop your ear. Eventually you won't need the chart.

Leads

Try this lead. It uses an A blues scale over a C major progression.

Let's analyze this next progression.

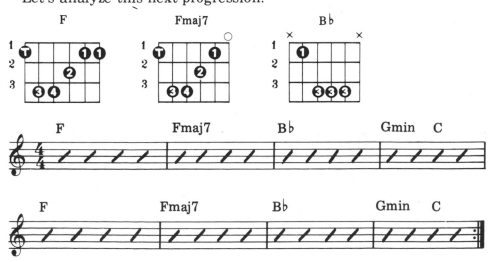

Play it through a few times. If you can, have someone play the chords for you while you try out different blues scales. This is a process you should always go through to develop your lead playing ability. Now let's consult the Blues Scales and Related Major Keys chart. What key contains all of the chords? What blues scale is related (three half steps down the chromatic scale)?

A D blues scale will work fine. The progression is in F major.

Use Fingering Two in first position and Fingering One in tenth position.

Combining Keys and Scales

Not all chord progressions lie conveniently within a major key. In fact, rock music often contains progressions that seem to be almost random collections of major chords. What should you play over these?

The answer lies in combining the two main ideas we've talked about.

By now you should have the sound of the blues scale in your head. But there are really two sounds. First, is the sound of the scale in its own key. We've used this against minor chords and seventh chords—for example, a G blues scale against a G7 or G minor progression. The second sound is the one we've just discussed, the idea of the relative major—for example, a G blues scale against a B♭ major chord progression.

The next chord progression is a common one in rock, used in such songs as *"Sympathy for the Devil,"* and *"Takin' Care of Business."* It has only major chords in it and they are not all contained in any one key.

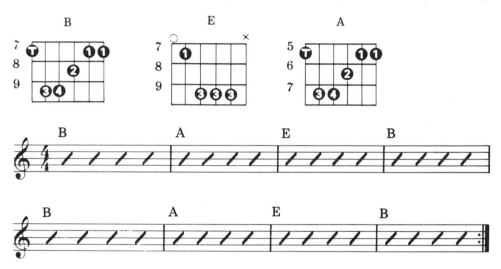

Play through the progression several times. You can tell that the home chord is B, but the progression is not completely in B major. The A chord is out of the key. We are going to use two scales to play lead. This will give us two sounds.

In the next example, the first eight measures will be a B blues scale lead. Then we will switch to the relative major and play a G♯ blues lead. These two sounds will take place over the same progression, the one we just analyzed.

This process is made somewhat simpler because both these scales may be played in the same position. In the first eight measures, the B blues scale will be played in seventh position, Fingering One. In the second eight measures, the G♯ blues scale will be played in seventh position, Fingering Two.

B blues scale, seventh position, Fingering One:

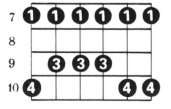

G# blues scale, seventh position, Fingering Two:

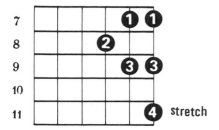

B blues scale:

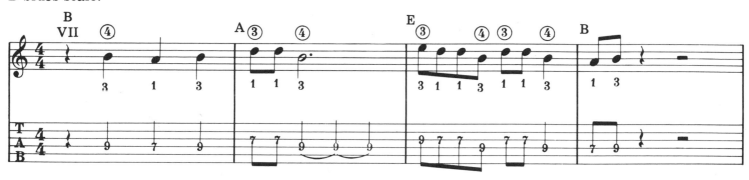

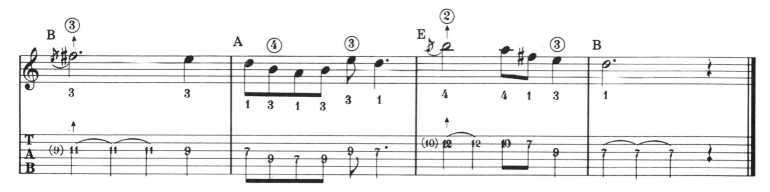

G# blues scale:

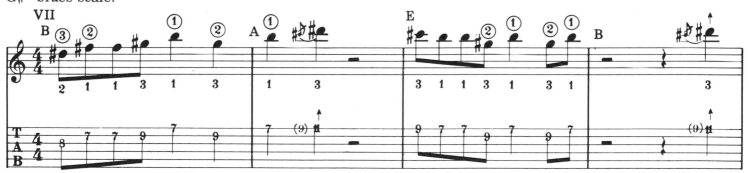

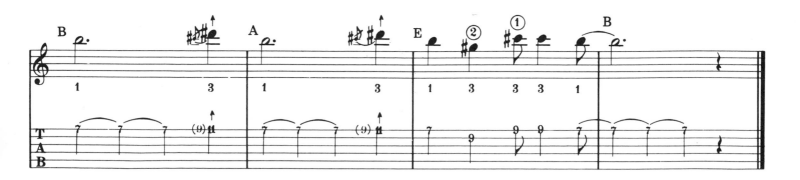

This technique of combining scales is very effective. It can be used in progressions that don't fall into one major key and it can be used even in progressions that are all in one key. You must learn to use your ear in determining what sounds *you* want to hear. The scales provide you with the raw material but you have to make it work.

In the next progression we see that most, but not all, of the chords fall within the major key of G. In constructing our lead, we'll use the G blues scale and the related blues scale of E. This time we'll freely move from one to another, so make sure you know both scales. In general, when you use Fingering One from one scale and Fingering Two from another, as in the chart below, the same position may be used. The chart shows how the combined notes from both scales look on the neck in third position. The circled notes are the notes from the E blues scale.

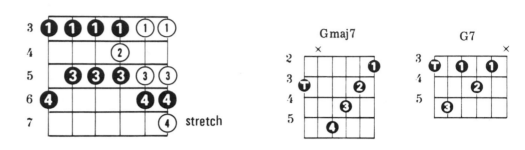

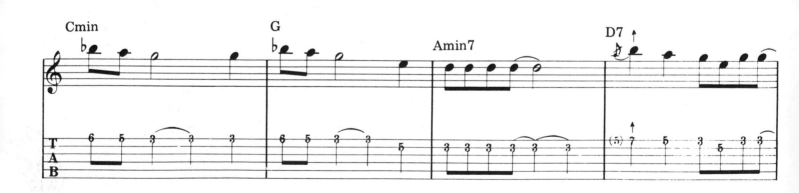

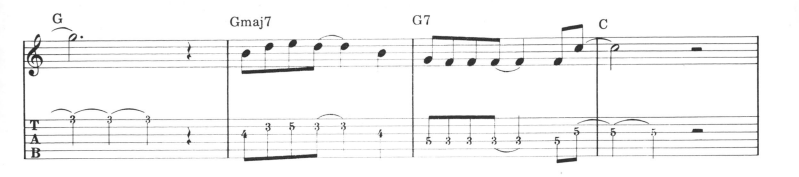

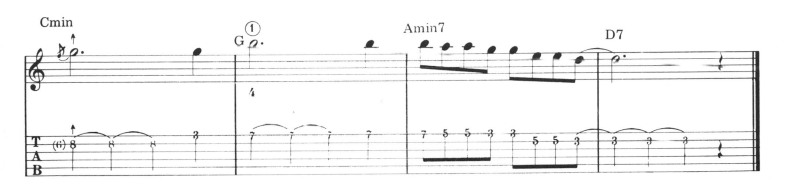

Jesse Colin Young

Pull-offs, Hammer-ons and Vibrato

There are a few more devices that, like bends, lead guitarists use to bring the notes alive. Let's take a look at three of these articulations that you can use to juice up your playing.

Pull-off

A *pull-off* is just what it sounds like. Finger the note with the left hand and pick it hard. Pull your left hand finger off the string immediately after you strike it. One note is picked, two are fingered and sounded. In the example below the Bb is fingered with the fourth finger on the first string. Right after picking the note, slide the fourth finger off and press down hard with the first finger on the G. That note is sounded without being picked.

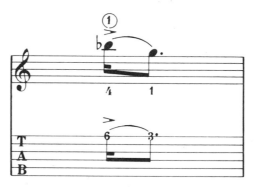

Hammer-on

A *hammer-on* is very similar in principal to the pull-off. Instead of striking a note and moving down in pitch to the next note, a note is plucked and "hammered-on" up in pitch. In the example below the F is fingered on the fourth string and picked hard with the right hand. The left hand's third finger is immediately hammered-on to the G on the fourth string. The note is sounded without being picked.

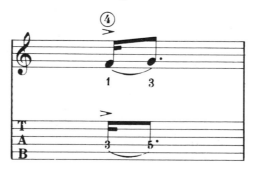

Both the hammer-on and the pull-off rely on strong finger pressure in the left hand. The action of the finger moving on the note (in the hammer-on) or off the note (in the pull-off) is what makes the note sound.

The next example uses these two devices. Use the G blues scale, third position.

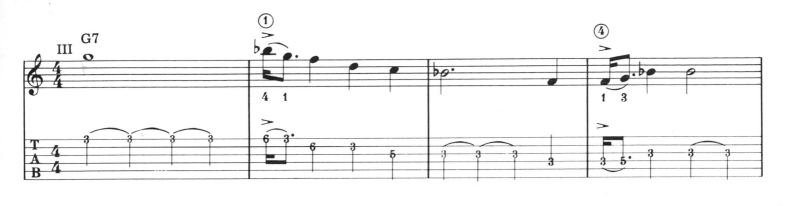

Vibrato

Like the bend, this is a very personal and expressive device. Some lead guitarists can be identified just from listening to the sound of their vibrato. A *vibrato* is a slight vibration of a note after it is struck. Press the note with the left hand finger, and take the rest of the hand off of the neck. Now, with only the finger playing the note on the fretboard, move the string up and down. This movement is in the direction of a line at right angles to the neck, not side to side as in a classical vibrato. This will be notated with a squiggly line (～～) over the note to be vibrated.

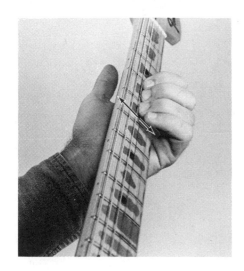

The next lead uses all the articulations we've talked about—vibrato, bends, pull-offs and hammer-ons. It's all over an Amin7 chord in fifth position, Fingering One.

Combinations

In our next lead we're going to combine some of the ideas we've talked about. The first two lines consist of a progression that is built around G minor. The G blues scale is the one we use. The first four measures are in third position, Fingering One. In the second four measures, we switch to sixth position, Fingering Two.

If you play the chords through several times, you'll hear that there's a very definite change in the sound between the first two lines and the second two lines. What has taken place is a modulation. A *modulation* is a change in key. We've gone from a G minor sound to an F major sound. (Look at the chart Blues Scales and Related Major Keys.) All the chords in the second part of the progression are related to F major which takes a D blues scale. We use Fingering Two in first position. Make sure to use the repeat signs so that you hear how this modulation fits together.

We're using all the articulations here—pull-offs, hammer-ons, bends and vibrato. Note that in the last line the hammer-on is combined with the vibrato. This is a very useful sound. Practice and get it down.

Playing in a Group

Most guitarists, no matter how much time they spend practicing on their own or playing with records, need the experience of playing with other musicians. This is especially true of the lead guitarist. All those beautiful licks you may be coming up with, and that great tone you've spent so much time working on—how great it would be to put it all together in a group. Well, don't just sit there, do it!

Chances are, nobody's called you up on the phone and invited you to come on down to the recording studio and record the album that will make you famous. So while you're waiting, get something together on your own. Anybody you remotely know who plays anything like the music you're into could be a start. Jam sessions are a great place to meet other musicians and find out if your abilities and expectations are similar. The point is, you should be playing with other people as much as possible in order to develop as a lead guitarist.

What exactly is the function of a lead guitarist? This of course will vary, depending on the other instruments and the kind of music you're playing. Basically though, the lead player should provide the group with color, orchestration and solos.

Color means, in music, a tone or a riff that adds another layer of interest to what is already going on, often in a way that does not draw too much attention. It may seem strange, but one of the hardest things for a musician to learn is when to just blend in. For example, if the drums, bass, and rhythm guitar are playing a chord pattern behind a vocalist, it is often sufficient to play very sparingly—a simple note pattern not too loud above the band, but with a tone on your guitar that will stand out somewhat or cut through the band without being too obtrusive. A tone device such as a phase shifter or wah-wah pedal is often useful here. This is coloration. Orchestration is a similar concept. Think of strings and horns and other added effects you may hear on records. They add punctuation and interest to the lead vocalist or main melody. In rock music the lead guitarist must perform this function sometimes single-handedly!

Let's look at some examples of color and orchestration-type parts that might be played in a group.

Think of this next example as a *vamp*: a chord pattern that is the introduction. It's played over and over again until the singer makes his entrance. In the vamp, the lead guitarist is playing a simple but characteristic melody. This melody might be doubled by another guitar, a piano, saxophone or by the bass guitar. The notes come from an A blues scale, fifth position.

Vamp

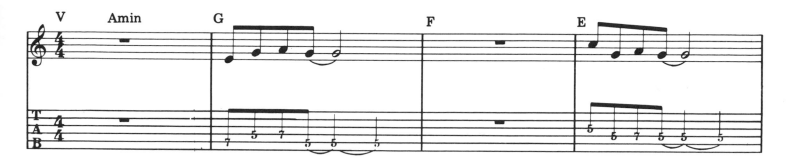

The lead guitarist is often called upon to *fill*: to play between the vocal phrases. Here, as in the vamp, simple characteristic melody lines are most useful—the kind that will stick in the head of the listener without cluttering up the music. Playing a lot of notes may show off your technique, but a musician should never lose sight of the basic beauty of the music as a whole. When filling, or in non-solo situations in general, the best players sublimate their egos to the whole blend of the sound. The time to burn is when you have a clear-cut solo spot, or maybe in a vamp at the end of a song where the most important thing is a loud, exciting climax.

Let's look at an example of filling in between a singer's phrases. This is a country-rock progression in C major. The notes come from the A blues scale, again, in fifth position.

Filling Behind a Singer

Double Lead

One technique of group playing that has excited a lot of guitarists in recent years is the *double lead*. The sound of two guitars playing a passage in harmony, with frequent bends, has been the characteristic sound of southern rock bands starting with the Allman Brothers, who gave birth to a whole new sound in rock guitar.

The sound is accomplished by having the two guitars play a melody in exact harmony and synchronizing the bent notes as closely as possible. This often means matching such effects as vibrato, pull-offs and hammer-ons, so you've got to work closely with your fellow guitarist. It is best to make the melody as simple as possible, especially at first.

I've written out an example below. We'll utilize the combined blues scales of G and E as discussed in previous chapters. The first guitar will also be switching positions, third and sixth, using Fingering Two in sixth position. There will also be a new bend as shown below. This bends the note E up to F, a half-step bend instead of the usual whole-step bend. This bend is in third position and combines notes from the two blues scales we are using. The E is from the E blues scale (Fingering Two, third position) and the F is from the G blues scale (Fingering One, third position).

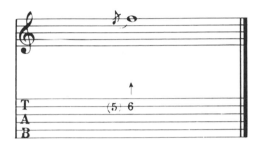

Steve Howe of *Yes*

Double Lead

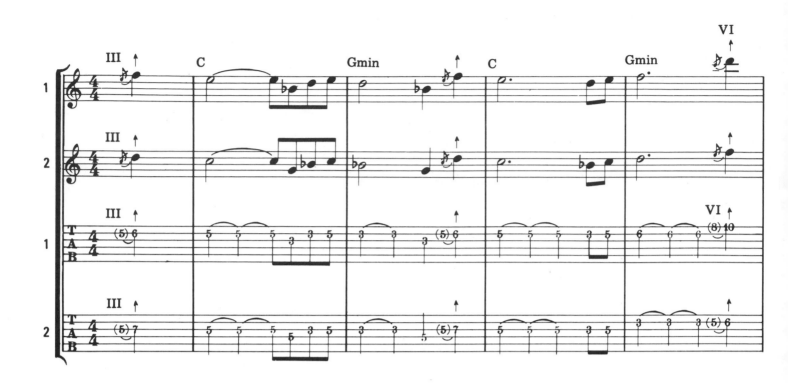

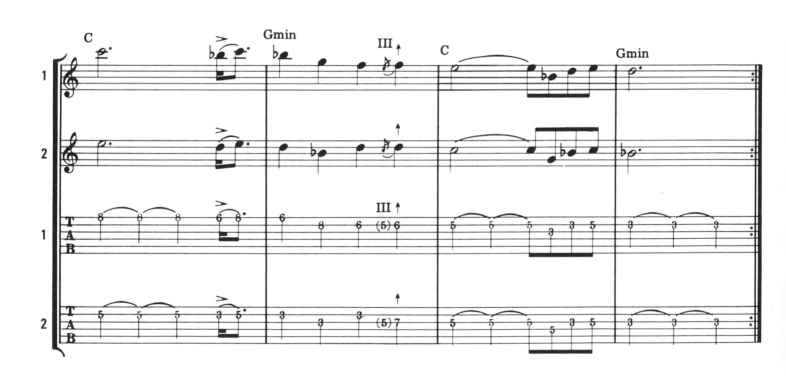

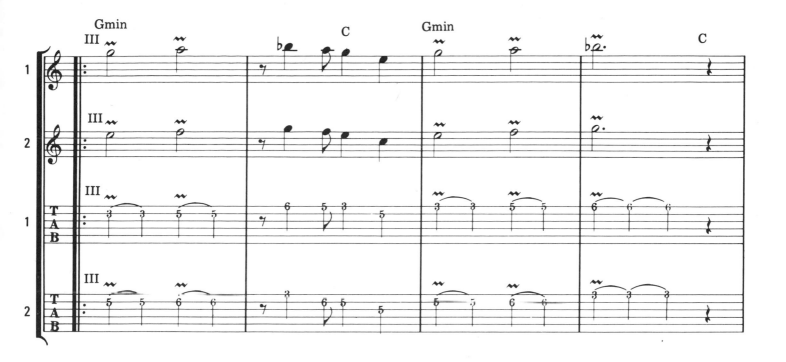

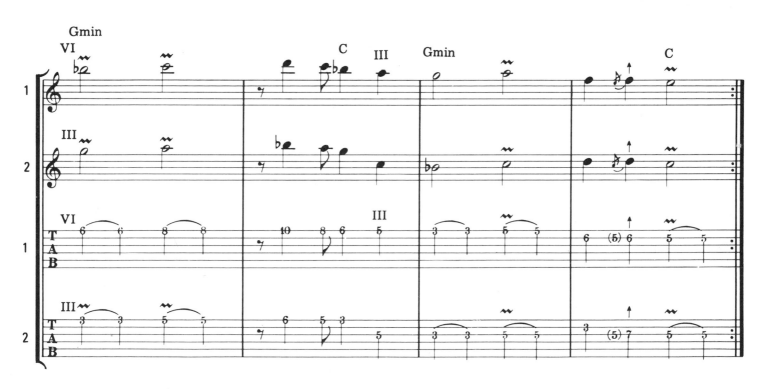

Afterword

You're now on your way to playing some good lead guitar. I hope you'll keep referring to the pages in this book and continue to go over the music until it's really a part of you. It's important to make up your own leads based on the things you've learned. Above all, keep playing and think about what you're doing. Playing with records is great, but the best practice of all is playing with other people as much as you can. Most of the exercises in this book work best with more than one player. They can even be played with a whole band. Just use the chords as the basis and go from there.

So keep growing, keep playing, keep learning and keep on rockin' and rollin'.

Jeff Beck

Discography

Listening to and playing along with records is one of the best ways that you can learn. Listen to anyone who turns you on, but here are some of the masters of lead guitar. With the help of a record player they can be your private teacher.

Chuck Berry
Early rock; still sounds great; inspired generations of rockers. *Chuck Berry's Greatest Hits*, Chess 1485.

B. B. King
The master of blues. *Live at the Regal*, ABCS 509.

Keith Richard
Mean, hard rock. Any Rolling Stones record, but my favorite is *England's Newest Hitmakers*, LL 3375.

Jimi Hendrix
The greatest lead guitarist who ever lived. Pioneer of modern rock sounds and, incidentally, an incredible blues player. True genius. *Are You Experienced*, R6261; *Axis: Bold as Love*, R6281; *Electric Ladyland*, RPS6307.

George Harrison
The perfect group player. Any Beatles record.

Eric Clapton
Turned blues into rock; pioneered the sound still imitated by ninety percent of lead players. *Blues Breakers*, PS492; *Disraeli Gears*, SD33-232.

John McLaughlin
The inventor of the fusion guitar; fastest gun in the West; inspiration from the East. *A Tribute to Jack Johnson* (a Miles Davis album), KC30455; *Birds of Fire* (Mahavishnu Orchestra), KC31996.

Jeff Beck
The master of flash and feedback. Very British and very good. *Truth*, BN26413.

Eric Gale and Cornell Dupree
The two top session guitarists in New York play their funk and R&B. *Stuff*, BS2968.

Your humble author may be heard (with Stan Bronstein and the Elephant Memory Band) on *Our Island Music*, MR5072.

Riffs and Chords for Guitar

Blues Riffs for Guitar
by Mark Michaels
This exciting new compendium gives you hundreds of riffs in the styles of all the major blues masters. By playing and using these riffs, the blues player can gain important insights into the theory and, more important, the feel of the music; how performers like Freddie King, Albert King, Buddy Guy, Otis Rush, Eric Clapton, Mike Bloomfield, and others get that true blues emotion into their playing. Useful for beginners as well as professionals. Chord changes for all riffs are included, plus performing hints and a discography. In standard notation and tablature.

Rock Riffs for Guitar
by Mark Michaels
This unique "how-to-build-riffs" approach for the electric guitar includes musical excerpts in the styles of Chuck Berry, Jeff Beck, Duane Allman and others. Special sections cover picking, fingering, bending, muting and hammering. Single and chordal riffs are all graded from easy to advanced. Discography included.

Jazz Riffs for Guitar
by Richard Boukas
Here is an important new book of guitar riffs in the styles of Django Reinhardt, Charlie Christian, Joe Pass, Wes Montgomery, Tal Farlow and others, arranged in order of difficulty. Each riff is presented with alternate fingerings for easy playing in different keys. A solo at the end of the book combines short and long phrases into a complete piece. Discography included.

Jazz Chords for Guitar
by Richard Boukas
Here is a complete dictionary of jazz chords as used by famous guitarists like Wes Montgomery, Joe Pass, Pat Martino, Django Reinhardt and others. Organized according to "chord families," the book includes material on how to construct chord melodies, and ways to connect chords through different positions.

Available at your local music store or directly from:
Music Sales Limited
8/9 Frith Street
London W1V 5TZ
Please add 50p per order for postage and handling.